
VIKING
Published by the Penguin Group
Penguin Putnam Inc., 375 Hudson Street, New York, New York 10014, U.S.A.
Penguin Books Ltd, 27 Wrights Lane, London W8 5TZ, England
Penguin Books Australia Ltd, Ringwood, Victoria, Australia
Penguin Books Canada Ltd, 10 Alcorn Avenue, Toronto, Ontario, Canada M4V 3B2
Penguin Books (N.Z.) Ltd, 182-190 Wairau Road, Auckland 10, New Zealand

Penguin Books Ltd, Registered Offices: Harmondsworth, Middlesex, England

First published in 1998 by Viking, a member of Penguin Putnam Books for Young Readers
Published simultaneously in Puffin Books

1 3 5 7 9 10 8 6 4 2

Text copyright © Harriet Ziefert, 1998
Illustrations copyright © Lisa Flather, 1998
All rights reserved

LIBRARY IN CONGRESS CATALOGING-IN-PUBLICATION DATA
Ziefert, Harriet.
Bugs, beetles, and butterflies / by Harriet Ziefert ; illustrated
by Lisa Flather.
p. cm.
Summary : Simple, rhymed text and illustrations introduce many
different kinds of bugs, beetles, and butterflies, including the
earwig, zebra butterfly, and water strider.
ISBN 0-670-88055-8 (hardcover). —ISBN 0-14-038691-2 (pbk)
1. Insects—Juvenile literature. 2. Beetles—Juvenile literature.
3. Butterflies—Juvenile literature. [1. Insects. 2. Beetles.
3. Butterflies.] I. Flather, Lisa, ill. II. Title.
QL467.2.Z45 1998 595.7—dc21   97–46912 CIP AC

Printed in Hong Kong
Set in Bookman

Viking® and Easy-to-Read® are registered trademarks of Penguin Books USA Inc.

Reading level 1.8

Contents

BUGS

Some bugs are pretty.
Some are ugly.

Some people hate
anything "buggly"!

5

Some bugs swim.
Most bugs fly.

6

Some can bite
and make you cry.

Bugs are fat.
Bugs are thin.

Some are skinny
as a pin.

Bugs suck blood.
Some smell bad.

Watching bugs
can make you sad.

11

Bugs creep.
Bugs eat leaves.

Some bugs even
act like thieves.

BEETLES

Beetles click.
Beetles dance.

Did you ever
have one crawl
up your pants?

15

Some are fast.
Some like mud.

16

Some even make
balls of crud.

Beetles eat pests.
Beetles eat mice.

Sometimes a beetle
doesn't smell
very nice.

BUTTERFLIES

Butterflies flit.
Butterflies flutter.

Butterflies can be
as yellow as butter.

Butterflies are mostly wing,
with lots of stripes and dots.

Look at all
the colors and
the many kinds of spots.

From the tiny egg
of a butterfly
comes a caterpillar,
which cannot fly.

It changes into a pupa.
And then one day...

a butterfly crawls out
and flies away.

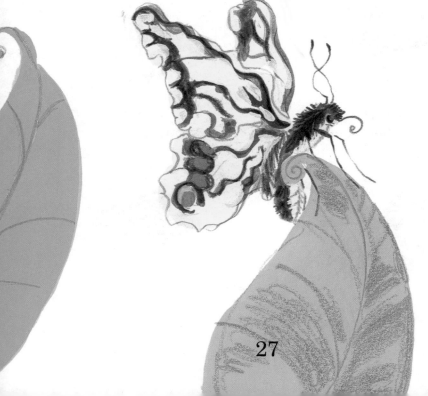

27

Insect Names

page 13:
Ambush Bug

page 20:
Arsalte Skipper

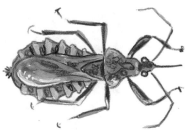

page 11:
Assassin Bug

page 4:
Band-Winged Grasshopper

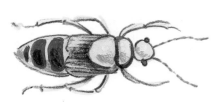

page 19:
Bombardier Beetle

page 8:
Bumblebee

page 20:
California Dogface

page 18:
Carrion Beetle

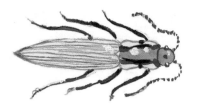

page 14:
Click Beetle

page 23:
Comma Butterfly

page 17:
Dung Beetle

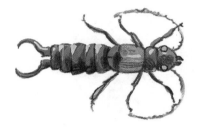

page 4:
Earwig

page 10:
Flea

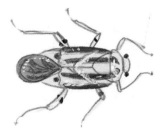

page 12:
Fourlined Plant Bug

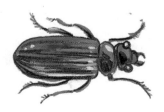

page 18:
Ground Beetle

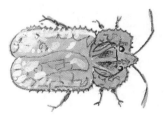

page 6:
Lace Bug

page 21:
Orange Sulphur Butterfly

page 20:
Reakirts Blue Butterfly

page 16:
Round Sand Beetle

page 16:
Rove Beetle

page 20:
Silvery Blue Butterfly

page 10:
Stinkbug

page 24, 27:
Swallowtail Butterfly

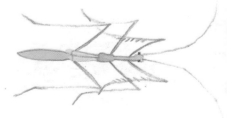

page 9:
Thread-Legged Bug

page 23:
Tiger Swallowtail

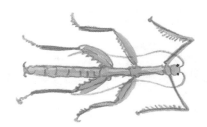

page 8:
Walkingstick

page 6:
Water Boatman

page 7:
Water Scorpion

page 12:
Water Strider

page 14:
Whirly Gig Beetle

page 22:
Wood Nymph Butterfly

page 22:
Zebra Butterfly

Science Fun

1. Watch a bug or a beetle. How does it move? How fast does it move? Can you move like a bug or beetle? Try it.

2. Touch a bug or a beetle. How does it feel? After it crawls or flies away, draw its picture.

3. Do you like bugs? Or do you dislike them? Write or talk about how you feel.

4. Do you know where a butterfly goes when it rains? Make up a story about a butterfly who finds a good place to keep dry.